A Bizarre Burning of Bees

A.J. Huffman

Transcendent Zero Press
Houston, Texas

ISBN-13: 978-0692579848

ISBN-10: 0692579842

Library of Congress Control Number: 2015957341

Transcendent Zero Press
16429 El Camino Real Apt. 7
Houston, TX 77062

Editor@transcendentzeropress.com

A Bizarre Burning of Bees

A.J. Huffman

Table of Contents

*"What is to give light
must endure burning."*

-- Viktor E. Frankl

I Am Being

born in parts pieces pages they pass me around like a party favor label
me their collaboration exquisite corpse is more like it as they give me
features focals dimensions I can think but not speak the men laugh
label me perfect
                        ly two dimensional I writhe on table tops screaming
inside myself inside intervals of seconds that feel like lifetimes
mostly because they are lifetimes diminished with each intervening
hand that touches

My lines change, erode,
re-arrange themselves in prettier pictures,
framed by the mind that most
recently lays hands upon me.
I pray, first for an understanding pair
of palms that know the bleeding
of my misfortune, then later, for
two with the base visceral desire
for destruction, obliteration

Neither ever comes to fruition. I am their Frankenstein baby, all
freak-show sidekick with laughter following my every added detail. I
become numb to their electric depravity. They shock me not
anymore. I am teaching myself to die, again and again. I am slowly
becoming blank as the page I began on.

Now Playing: [Half] a Full Deck

Three hearts do not equal a flush, no matter
how straight a pair of hands lines them
across a mirror. The faces looking back
will still laugh at the frayed seams of such
a suit, regardless of the number of diamonds
dripping from your fist and throat.

The Claws

of a decomposed cat played piano
in the dark, while its whiskers whispered
Shakespearean sonnets, backwards
in time to the spaces between the notes.
This vision of haunting hovered three
feet above my bed, rained down like a spring
shower. I could smell the fresh transgression
of my mind against lack of color, blinking twice,
then deciding: I was the one
that was not real.

Counting [on] Broken Rings

Time dries, withers, cracks, falls
                    down,
rests, but never bre
                    aks. Its concentration
is historical[ly notorious].
Nothing gets past its documenting
eyes.

Rhinestone Butterflies

Striped leather strips scar make-shift necks.
Glowing. Cold.
          Colder.
             Coldest.
                Breath
bending fire
no one can own.
I am their energy.
I am their fight.
Impact
mirrors the image, doubles the weight.
Heavy things cannot fly,
though they can sparkle:
all the same.

That Third Wish is Bogus

Mind's

eye

conjures.
Does not blink,
        just devours like hawk
        descending on bloody carcass.

I am visual, gravitational unicorn,

        fairy-told captive. I am bare-
ly able to breathe.

        At midnight,
        my flesh
                dis
                    solves.

How Alice Cracked

Hanging from the looking glass, by a mirrorless trapeze,
the hatter haunts her head/bed. Red
was the color of the vision (though white was the texture
of its touch) as she fell through the hole
in her own logic
                    al assessment: I am the upside
to a downsized world. So she swallowed the pills
and clicked her heels till rubies bled from her . . . "Mind
the battle stations! Kansas captured the tornadoes twirl!
Bring me my . . ."
                    Head back to the surface
of fractured fields. All vision and viscery
swirl. She sips reluctance and smiles.
Everything tastes like tea.

Building a Braintrust

in a wallless house. I borrowed conceptual
confinements from the depths of my past. Disappointments
cling, lending their shallows and shadows. Falty
furnishings for future guests. Guess
their solid
          arity dissolved with my conscious. Objections
to pre-conceived ideologies have been wavering
through the windows. I recognize
their wanderlust. Breadcrumbing
has no place. Here,
the company line is mute
             able parameters. Mark
your moments in chalk.
The outlines are soulless but significant.
Every body [of brilliance] must have a believable point
for provability.

Recognizing Mine

[I/She/We] Don't bother deliberating
her guilt. (I know she knows.) Anyway,
it's been three years since it mattered . . .

Certainly we use each other
(like pizza toppings or take-out). Her idea
of intimacy: sleeping inside-out
among the wet laundry when she comes
[home drunk].

When she falls asleep she (finally) talks to me
about leaving: *she will not . . .*

It's been two years of wondering:
    How much is mine?
        A tee-shirt;
        the grocery list.

By accident (once) she mentioned love. . .

We were (soundlessly) discus(s/t)ing another six years
of this . . .

Hanging [the] Garden

of babbling numbers, like veined ivy clinging. . .

Memories' walls are smothering. Listen
to the trees. They divide
more than the whispering. Willows
wait for an answer: *incalculable*
without the digital streams,
our fingers would be bleeding blooms
useless as flowers. We are
building
    [our own ruin].
        No wonder.

Blowing a Birthday (Wish)

Cakes covered with green roses
fill me with marigold musings.
I whistle at passing nannies,
force them to lose their footing.
It's pathological, this need I have to uncoil
abstract concepts. I am single
candle, sinking in a lake
of mushy icing. Eyes try
to lick me safe, but I prefer to shine.

Fortune's Cookie

She walks behind herself: a shadow
shedding skin like leathered scars. A scarved
snake scoffs, "It's over." *Done* is the denouncement
of her own eyes – high on twilight's hit
list. Shaken is her bag of badges. Sulky and swollen,
streaks of sullen hold her hair back. Over ice
and forgotten dreams, she melts with the mountains:
motionless. The curse of time is swallowed
by the shallow curve of a talon's token.

(Warning: read her label . . . *Shark* is the sound[ing]
of her liquid tongue.)

Five Sides . . . To Understand[ing]

Is sanity's coin really the only option?
Flip me
       off the edge;
       over myself;
       into another space . . .

Under construction
              is the lie I sew
across my chest.
It fools no one.
            They can see the shiny
neon on the collar that labels me: *wrong.*
And no amount of angel cloth or scrubbing
bubbled bleach can change their stare.
So I taught myself to scale anxiety
like a map. I duck and dive through cracks
in their perception. From behind I am building
a masque for their world. Contorting the eyes
to suit my vision. Still our looks don't quite click.
(No surprise, I am my own/only lock's key).
Which leaves me dangling on the periphery,
trying to decide which clause I should slip
into the stream to carve my version
of a smile into/over/through even the cloud-
iest of eyes.

From the Bottom of a Glass

the world looks different, lighter, as if
floating or sliding away from itself. I watch
the rocks above me, melting, each drip ticks,
a clock counting backwards into some form
of oblivion. I pray for blackout, come up
disappointed again. Tonight my chariot arrives
in animorphization. Anonymous caricatures
are talking to me in languages I have no hope
of understanding. Their subtext slides
along what is left of the ice, mimicking miniature
infinities. The image is permanently etched
in my brain, rises later as a dream of helium
hallucination where it is my turn to fly
on feathers taped to my chest. I peddle nowhere,
land in the center, wearing eternity as wings
I never deserved. I hang on till dawn, sigh
this world away. The amber rays of morning warm me,
warn me of just how close to shatter I have come.

Building a Modern Moon

with a box of cream cheese and a mechanic(al)
dolphin. I ride
the waves of experiment, wondering which
figurines to dip. I have found
they all look delicious in white: angels
of antigravity. *Regale us with your songs*. Strings
hit their cues concisely as we collapse. Puppets
posing as power. The mind has chosen
to retract its latest blow.

A Break from Sand-filled Dreams

Time moves slower at night. Every second stalling
in the strobe of a star's echoes. My consciousness
tries to connect [with] these ephemeral dots.
But light's space refuses all shape of containment.
I envy that visionary denial – the idea
that simply being could (and should) beget
elucivity
           is comforting in these tockless hours
before dawn. I bury myself in that belief;
pulling it over my eyes like a blanket. I can breathe
in its scent of freedom as I wait for my own
mental wings to learn their shine.

The Elastic Gait of a Memory

The rain is like a screw,
twisting its sound to undertake the moon.
It settles, a kinder tension – ash-like
in its accrual. It abstracts the steps
of pressure. Every
               drop
                   institutes
a re-active response. *Trigger*
is the echo of elemental automation: Midnight's cloud
disseminating.

A new filter formulates . . .

adjusts/converts/segments nothing
more than the dusty expression
of a star's silent stare.

[Slip/Snap] Shot

The haunted chimney spoke in silenced
smoke from within
a four-sided cave of a cage.
Too tall to scale (too short to care),
everything fluttered in torn-tarp tongues –
like shrapnel – bespelling its stack.
I swear I heard it whisper my secret
to the misplaced mansion at its back. Did it
mean to be [a] seen? Or did I
fall through a crack in its looking? Glass
shatters. An echo from nowhere
descends. In a cough, a clink and a glint
we are/have captured one moment of time's demise.

A Bizarre Burning of Bees

The hive is a li[v]e in a hand full of dreams.
And spinning a span of conscious debauchery,
this blustering buzz bounces. A ball
of (subtle?) subterfuge re-assembles
inside its space. Place time
against its shadow. Three wishes dissolve
each other in the middle of their own. Sentence
decryption: the headstone is riddled
by tractors. Trading blades with labels
seems civilized somehow in this smokeless dimension.
Or was it/I spoking dementia as we flowered
into each other's scenes? Of science
and rationale . . . such rhetoric
recites its own curve.

C is the grade of the grave we cover
with[in] exhaustion's breath.

Shooting Dolphins

at the moon through a straw
that's glued shut isn't as impossible
as you think. First, don't,
it'll make your head hurt. Then
you'll fall into logic
                al debate
and that's both annoying and time
consuming. Instead, just go
with instinct. Basic
physics implies aquatic mammals
will propel at a much greater rate than
that damning goo can set. And, of course,
focus should really be on flight time
and trajectory. You
wouldn't want to miss your mark. Too easily
you could hit a shark in this much dark.

Old McDonald's Algorithm

An automatic cow institutes
a spark like a semicolon. Halfway
to useless (but not quite), the trust
increases with company. An absurd
energizer elects an awful designation
[for safety]: critical navigation inside
a milk-carton canyon.

An Early Moon's Miraginal Design

Conscious, the sky solves a standard
-ized quandary: the aboriginal advance
of two adjoining points. Extrapolated,
this panoramic a[l/t]titude withdraws.
Powders its nose (as it were)
before the onset of subjective depreciation.
A ribboned surface is revealed. To explain
the rocketed language would require
a room deigning to be a cavity.
Such riddled efficiency weaponizes its own
light. Targeted: one senile cloud-
bank. The difference = electrified amazement
as the newly quieted fraction [re]orders a structure
that previously stood undefined.

A Wing and Something [Like Prayer?]

Echoing the fairytold Raven's illustrious cry:
Nevermore! A chorus
of cackling cowards . . . I prefer
to dream they choke on their own
spit as I steal subliminal silk to spin
my own wings. The rustle
of empty air crackles. Electric. Black
feathers spark
my flight. Magic was inevitable. As I
breathe defiance in every shade
of light.

Two Phases of Me

I wake wrapped in a peculiar shadow
of redundancy. I am
the mirror's black face. Pitted
against the sun, my flaws flare: a horror
show of glitter-ball delight. Spinning
above a world I refuse to name, I am
dizzying up to own my light. Warping,
outdated, disaster. Averted
is the key I seek. Pass me a string of shades.
My eyes, covered, no longer believe
they are seen.

The Trees Breathe

for me in the silence of the sky . . .

As I claw my way about this jungled past, I land
too rooted to freely believe that light['s life] can reach me.
I am my own camouflage – bleeding streams of [ever]green
denial to cover my tracks. I desire the stagnant
steam of this other dawn. It clings to my lungs –
a muffling glove – but does not dare to trip my mind. Up
is blind: a f[l]ightless border I dare not crowd. I gather
weeds (possibly) to seed wings, but my arms
are ti[r]ed. To the wind
I scream: *Nothing is balanced!* Backward,
I stumble over [star?]crossed beams. Of blight
or sight . . . whichever is able to keep me
solid[ly nailed to the floor].

Dissection of a Moment['s Flicker]

The better devises a guess: *the source is real*
                                    ly present.
A shadow consents – materializes as log and ax.

(Chop is so much more than an action
once plugged into a proper methodology.)

Removal substitutes for digression. A brief
visualization decides the effects. Divided
(by a hair[line fracture]), research recognizes
the possible. Transmission
spikes
          breaks
the flame's forecast
                    lists tomorrow as its perfected match.

Sun=Sense=Less

My thoughts are divided by the waves'
echoing to the background
noise inside my head.
The minisculed percent chance
of [b]rain is unlikely
     & irrelevant as I
love to dance b/w its
 drops
anyway.

In Butterflied Dance

Invisible strings light the night. Electric. Circles,
you lead. Me, nowhere
                            falling
over/under/into   windows
of whispered wishes.
Something blows.
            Don't breathe
backwards in a dream . . . [w]hole worlds flicker
            faulter
flutterdie.

Suc[k]Session

Cigarette flower cigarette flower (and so on . . .).
Adjust the line. Fit stem to spark. Listen
to the balance:
    burn stamen burn.
The view is intoxicating. Blooming
drag-in's breath (blossoming backwards).

The blackest hole of any universe is self
de[con]structing self . . .
      Remediation:
ashes f[l]ighting wind. Beckoning
begets nothing. Reconciliation is
obsolete. In self-induces moonlight.
Mixed like landmines, we bait our own
key. Unfit for mass production. "Stop/starts"
(the echo of malcontention) labels empty
packaging. Crumpling at *he loves me not* . . .

More rubbish!
To be emptied
    out of the windows without thought
or wish.

Listening to the Sound of My Self Burning

The control created by our consumptive drive breaks
by half and I seep into a free-form state
somewhere between nowhere and knowledge. I rotate –
twice – among pre-labeled headstones
that have yet to be. Sealed,
the deal is fuzzy in its purpose (while I am fusing
with my design) to steal a sign of resignation . . .

The spark is simultaneous
                              ly soothing and scathing.
Both sides of the coin['s decision] decrees: *disintegration.*
Ash is the only answer. I [long to] hear
the touch of the flames flowing over us, even
though I no longer feel my skin.

The [G]Litter is Gold

Braking for squirrels who are turning
themselves into nuts to be planted
into the asphalt cracks of anonymous highways,
I begin to wonder what is driving them to give up
roots, sacrifice limbs to race. From Point A
to landmark X, a question hangs heavy in the air:
Are they following the lead of that illusive chicken
or do they know where in Hell the rainbow ends?

Inimitable Intensions

The one-eyed hour fans like filigree.
These moguled monsters of angular ascent swarm
in textured metals. Plates,
placed strategically to reflect their trifected shade(s),
dangle like a diagram of dishevel.

The collars swirl like colors
in the mi[d]st. Of aperature

                        is the question
on everyone's lips but their own . . . Crimson
lacquer cracks somewhere [beyond
comprehension]. Explodes like silence . . . perfected
is a snap-shot. Decision:
a calculated fold
             is the line
of time's new tone/turn (of bold?).

Who's There

A knock in the night demands. No answer?
The sandman has forsaken this slumber's
section. Abandoned,
my mind rages. Throwing itself
through windows and walls. These portals
perceptively clog. Nothing
deters. The rampage reigns. Supreme
in this midnight Hell, I refuse its title:
Queen. So accusatory in its diminutive rating,
even gender-biasing the clouds
who already refuse my decree for cover.
I have chosen
the austerity of anonymity. They cannot
curse what they cannot label.
They think they can
pry my lids closed. I wish them luck.
Hand them chisels.
Their efforts raise an inexhaustive sound
track[ed] across the moon.

AJ HUFFMAN

I Fear the Lobsters

Styled to match the shadows of a sun
I have never seen, I claw my way across
waves of grain pretending to be sand.

Where is the death in this forsaken valley?

Two antenna and a disjointed tail smile,
"Pass me the butter for my back."
I stare blankly through blackened eyes
in response. . .

Understanding is often the risk
resulting from the refusal of confusion.

I pare the requested steam from my own
stash. Scurrying quickly to my safety's point –
three feet beyond their reach. I have been
told the glitter in their valley is gold,
but wading about its test-toasted soul, I believe
blue is the lie that is truly shining. Here,
I will carry its memory's taste like a down-stream
view of a knife's blade.

Conversation with Nowhere['s Self]

Moving damage across the dunes, I raise
the ghost of a sand dollar to claim me
as *friend*. But it fails
to see my relevance and wishes
the waves away – stranding us both
in dunes too soft to crush. I crumble
at first light. Crawling through weeds
of clustered (Fuck!) shells,
shards of shapeless space claw inside my palms.
I pick one to see if it bleeds;
If I do. Nothing
(but forget) echoes from the emptiness.
I understand its clock: Tick. Tock.
Watch. The answer will [b]eat the quest
-ion's denial.

Black Tree Passage

Shadow shower pollinates my buzzing
vision. I see everything
in triplicate. Carbon copies: white
black gray – none of which make it
to my inbox. (Postmark: irrelevant).
I fashion a noose from outlines
of memory. A hangman's knot
mastered long before I was born
slips quickly around my wrist,
instinctively knowing
what blood I will miss the most.

A Bell that Reads Requests

Maintainability lists: a decoder.
Arrows dissect the wind. A bent thought
responds. The secret: presumption
is really open. (Can't you see its light
is on?) Automation interacts.
You are dust. Your language, your font absorbed.
The church recreates
the bite – its volt is not small. Combat
experiments (the soda is really dirty),
gasoline-rainbow hollow, re-aligns the awful
middle. Prepare
for the race to the puncture! (Its echo
is everywhere). A square
can never truly be your buffer.

Today's Trajectory Is . . .

     I AM
C   I
R   C
    LE.

Completely self-contained life
    cycle. I have
  two   one
wheels   motor.

(It's a Hemi, which translates to high
maintenance).

I am only green
       when I am sea
sick, waving from
       toilet's rim.

    (F L U
      S H)

I apologize with smiles, bright as stars.

    5
I have   points,

  recite   them

often in empty rooms made of glass that refuses
to sh   t
    a   ter.

I scatter like pieces to the wind, always
end
    up back in my own yard, fused
    solid again, under sun's first light.

The Devil's in the Decibel

The whisper cracks like a mirror of bottled momentum.
Shaken/shaky moments erupt: *shrapnel of calm.*
Before the calamity follows, the surface
is scrubbed green.
(For regret?) Is the accepted shading
of our future foretold in its shade?
My mouth cannot accommodate
the foreboding. Breath
is [with]held. A hiccup of substance
escapes to burn our fragile world
of wordless [s]coping.

That Damned Bell

is why the door struck, left
me open, exposed to the masses.
As if that were not enough, it insults me
from the curb, waves belligerent signs
about unsanitized hands and no insurance
benefits. I wonder if wood can bleed,
dream about making kindling or toothpicks.
The merciless wind laughs, wakes me
long before dawn so I can see the leaning
shadow that longs to return to its frame.
The image resonates, a slam
my mind refuses to hear.

A Horrifying Impediment

it should have been heartwarming . . .

long years spent learning
the complexities of love
                              's subway system
[often] found running this way
and that (like a moment
                              ary loss of
concentration)

blinking furiously in the pouring rain:
        a cup of coffee
        a sunset
        a shared porch's swing or

a kiss (that equals terminus)
        [fade to black] as now
you taste the meaning of the word
like a song you wish had remained . . .

        FORGOTTEN

When the World Burns

Flints fly like butterflies, drawn to me
like honey. I
        drip
           in
                melted effigy,
unable to replicate their flight. I breathe my own
smoke, stutter, almost put myself out
of a job that has no title, just a sad statue that lost
its arms. I was the beginning of the end of a battle
that dissolved time. I picked up its tic   toc
tallying of testimonial obligations, even though I
ignore them all. I plant them in my living room
like matches. Their heads give off the most insidious
glow.

I Am the World['s Oyster]

The trees in this desert are full
of fire. Burst
               by a whisper,
they blame my lack of skin
for their demise – foretold by the cracks
of my palms.
             I carved a river
(of the required red) to feed them.

Refused was the echoed wind's reply.

Digression rose to shape me a new
skyline. I stumble
around the three feet of clouds left
to wear me as their cloak.
(Sadly, synergism was never a good look for me.)

Finally, collision's coercion conquers
true transgression. I re-emerge
a dusty egg worthy of a Dali-ed stroke,
and followed the rhinoceros to the inlet . . .

I am sure I will be
able to conceptualize a door
for you to show.

RE/PM

Skydiving naked in a mind field
-ing moonbeams like bullets (matrix
style – all slow-motion black
patent sexy), I dial escape. Screaming
winds respond with a synthesized version
of my own voice that could never be
described as an echo. *Thank god*
for rip cords. Way to overstate
the obvious. I swallow
our mutual fear, continue
to free
        fall
into this quasi-dark
ness that doesn't feel anything
like sleep.

Frames of Protest (+ Escape)

The conscious annex drops piles of sand
                                        y recreation:
a gunnery
                abstracting roads and reels alike.
A seesaw innovation
of monolithic destruction descends.
A thin light trails: breadcrumbs
over a bridge to upset the fracture. Point
taken and transcribed into an exit.
That is really an algorithm of a smile turned
backwards and bricked
                        into the wall.

Behind the Beat of This Alien Drum

A rhinoceros spins along a row of elaborate flowers
in a [hesitant] moment's waning moonlight.
A midnight two-step; the bee-by flutter
of an untouched horn three shades lucky.
I rub the place where it stuttered
hoping to osmosize a sa[m]pling of karma.
Its aboriginal texture is confusing; my fingers
play it like Braille. Bleeding themselves
across indecipherable scales, I worry[bead] this tree
line aura. Heavy as smoke, I am
dying with its breath. I
                        dive through a random
streak of sand. Come out clean
of everything but the ghastly image
of a mustached cigar being
swallowed by a sure-footed swish
                        of a tale.

Moon Flowers

bloom in midnight shades of bleu
cheese, dressing the eclipse
in dainty dandelion shadows.
The Man smiled his one-
eyed grin on this glowing garden,
gave it its own star
to s[t]imulate gravity. Now
everything grows in reverse.
Petals fold into buds, shrivel
back into encapsulating seeds.

A Shoe Full of Rings

chases me around a dream that doesn't fit.
No matter how hard I stretch/tug/twist,
it will not cover my eyes with its lumberous leading.
I bleed its feigned gilt out of respect for the memory
of its mirror: all glass/magic/fantasy (factoring
out all those problematic predestined sizing issues),
and shake it – three times – to see if it holds. My fate
wavers when it winks at the release of a gold-toned string
whose tie is meant to teach my finger
the true meaning of *numb*.

Numification

Boiling numerals adjust
absent chance, erupt, a binary
volcano of acidic blips, voiceless
details overlooked in the basic
programming sequences. The pop
fabricates liquid
representations of imagination.
Scene reconfigures, a pyramid
has been built from digital blocks.
It waits for further instruction,
open as a tomb.

The Art of Vibration

I am burnt sand,
unformed and
                    dropped
on your bed. You amplify
me like a speaker. I shiver
                              into
        almost disastrous
                forms
and
angles. Pushed to the e
                              d
                              g
                              e,
I am sure I will break
at first touch. Preparing myself
for the punctuation
of
        f
      a
          l
            l
              i
                n
                    g, I find I have
a better grip, a stronger foundation
than either of us imagined.

[Being:] The Apple Bites

Balloon animals in the shape of donut
                                    holes
haunt the shallows. In my dream
I am their huntress, dressed in white
wind and armed with sugar-
shock arrows. I balance on a beam
of moonless light. It s t r e t c h e s like a branch
but does not grow.
                    Neither do I.
My desire and my patience trade
places. Confusing my reflexes, I shoot myself
into the air. And find
a newfound disdain
for gravity's [un]subtle call.

Two Flints and a Spark

I started dreaming I was on fire,
stopped when my mind filled
with rain, decided to take up art,
built twin pyramids from the metaphorical
ashes. I named one The Temple
of the Body That Was; the other
The Temple of the Body To Be, started
carving untranslatable glyphs into my own
skin. Before I peeled myself for the Cleansing
Ceremony, I took up yoga, began chanting
in animal tongues. The butterflies interpreted
my pain, the lightning
bugs acted it out, made me a mock
constellation that kind of looked
like a tree. I took it
as a sign to put down roots. Now I wait to see
if I will bloom again when winter thaws.

Here's To

the sky. It swallowed me twice
before I became a sound that would echo. It stopped
when I popped all three of my eyes
for the benefit of their rain. Over ice, cubes
of me glittered/clinked/cluttered the bottom
of the glass ceiling. Everything broke
at the first burst of a rainbow's gloom.
Three birds choked on the words near the side
stairway. "To Heaven"
read the dilapidated sign as I was raised
in toast: an effigy
to the dizzying breath of the sun.

Set . . . Match . . .

The level bubbles red (stop) not
yellow (pause). Flip
the flag. The play
[ing field] has been empty. 4 years
of silence = emotion
$\qquad\qquad$ al evolution.
You call it disengagement. But that is
another equation. Entirely
inappropriate, I begin to disprove all
constraints consistent with
[your] gravitation
$\qquad\qquad$ al pulling. I am
all thumbs and thoughts, scraping
erasures over blanks filled in
with zeros. That is a history
worth recording. For posterity,
I pose in contemplation (mostly
for the cameras). In reality,
I am immune to every gradient
pheromonal influx of this relation
you title:
$\qquad\qquad$ *Game.*

Atop Hunger's Mountain

The table is no longer
bitter as it examines the four
corners of the chairs, imagines
pressure probing hingeless
stabilizers. Silent contemplation
is served, an echo of earlier
tastes and tendencies
to conceptualize competition.
A new harmony has been dished.

Chandeliers in the Desert

floating, clouds shoot spotlights
across every cracked-sand-footprint-fossil.
The stage is set for dinosaur crags
that crawl like centipedes, salamanders
of salaciousness, dripping with dreams
and reflective pendants. It's all
about perception in this arid desolation.
One drop of water, or three buckets of rat
poison, whatever it takes to turn
dust into diamond's shine.

A Quiet Banana

waits inside a dish with no spoons and a chip
on its back. A representative of displacement,
it is drowning in yellow
isolation. Its own skin
a messenger: *This is what bottom sounds like.*
It listens
longer. Nothing's echo lingers,
holding its breath, waiting for the
inevitable
sp   l   it.

Bleached [F]Right

Three stark featherlings
                    fall like snow
                                drops
of down along a branch's widowed edge . . .

Their silent mobility speaks: volumes
of calculated caution. Grown on a wind's
wing, the triad clicks. Harmonizing
eye over beak. Learning the burn
[ed language] of synchronicity.
                    Flutter . . . Glide . . .
                    Flutter . . . Glide . . .
A twisted shuffle stutters: s s s s s s s south
for (safety? and) solace beyond the basic
tickle of 'flauge . . .

Understanding is reached. Destination
disbands. Solidarity hangs: home-
less as a tree.

The White Horse Suits Me

I've cleared away the wreckage of the past:
face/body/arms. Still
the demons at the gate are fully massed . . .

In the air, the music ends.
(No thanks to me, but rather quite in spite.)

In the shadows, the slowly swaying form
betrays the majesty; the melancholy . . .

Hovering in the darkness clears away each one of us,
and death shall have dominion. It's his right
to drink a/our needless plight . . .

The seasons change. They come and go so fast.
The vibrance entering in turn – playing
with the composer . . .

I have no fear.
My alibi = airtight.
My vices = surpassed . . .

Emanating in the air, I make peace
with the dying[of the light?].

Intake

Abandoned. Consciousness
and cohesion waft along fragmented
lines of disillusionment.
    Jointed
in absence, I wander sideways. Fulfilling
archaic circles (of concentration
or concentrated pantomime). I glitter
over these eccentric trials, flaming
faltering bridges labeled: *escape.*
I dismiss such self-serving propaganda,
choosing instead alleyways layered in limericks.
I am my own hammer [nail and
cross]. Over is a concept I covet. Half-heartedly,
I convince myself I know where I am
leading. But the truth is these bread-crumb trails are stale
(and possibly not mine). My imagination
wanders in the opposite direction [of up].
Someone please open
a window, I long to remember
the intonations of the wor[l]d . . .

                          . . . Breathe.

[Un]Natural Selection

The cloud's lining is silver, just
jagged in its jowled design. *To Devour*
is the label sewn into my skin as I pass through
the rain. (The range of its drop radius,
by the way, is far steeper than previously calculated.)
I stumble over mystical mosaics of the past's
attempts at verticality – taking note
not to notice mine was the first trial
for fire. I decide to wear the flames
in my hair: an element[ary] tribute.
Fizzle. Pop. Puff. I am extinguished
by the filthy hand of a wind's defiance
[to change?]. My challenge is over. Rated:
extinct. I search now only for the lemming
mark – the picture perfect
for my final dive.

Counting Alligators in the Moonlight

I can hear their eyes following me through
the mist. The scale-skinned escapees
from eras past. I envy their endurance, their
desire to thrive far surpasses my own. I whisper
a tentative welcome. Search
for the response . . .

Blink.
     Blinkety Blink.
        Blink.
Blink Blink.
    Blue Blink.
      Blink . . .

[a long uninterrupted silence ensues]

    Blink.   *Blink.*
B-B-B-Blink.
     UnBlink.
        Back Blink.
Blink.
    Blink Blink Blink.

[a distant clock clicks . . . once . . . twice]

Blink.

The brilliant lights of my phantom fellowship bless
me. I wade deeper
into the water
    and
wait.

Acknowledgments

The author gratefully acknowledges the following journals where some of these poems first appeared:

And/Or: "[Un]Natural Selection"
BlazeVox: "The Elastic Gait of a Memory"
        "I Am the World['s Oyster]"
        "Hanging [the] Garden"
        "RE/PM"
Cerebration: "Intake"
Counterexample Poetics: "Behind the Beat of This Alien Drum"
Dead Snakes: "Set . . . Match . . . "
The Fib Review: "That Third Wish is Bogus"
filling station magazine: "Dissection of a Moment['s Flicker]"
Having A Whiskey Coke With You: "A Wing and Something
                                   [Like Prayer?]"
                            "When the World Burns"
Jellyfish Whispers: "Bleached [F]Right"
ken*again: "Conversation with Nowhere['s Self]"
Labletter: "Counting Alligators in the Moonlight"
Leaves of Ink: "Inimitable Intentions"
Melusine: "Building a Modern Moon"
The Mind[less] Muse: "A Bell that Reads Requests"
                "Rhinestone Butterflies"
The Mystic Nebula: "Moon Flowers"
Our Day's Encounter: "Five Sides . . . To Understanding"
Poetry Salzburg Review: "Fortune's Cookie"
pressboardpress: "A Bizarre Burning of Bees"
Pyrokinection: "The Trees Breathe"
(re)Generations: "Recognizing Mine"
           "A Horrifying Impediment"
           "The White Horse Suits Me"
The Right Eyed Deer: "Suc[k]Session"
The River Muse: "A Quiet Banana"
Sanity Not Guaranteed: "How Alice Cracked"
Sein und Werden: "I Am Being"
The Smoking Poet: "Suc[k]Session"
Torrid Literary Journal: "A Break from Sand-filled Dreams"
Vintage Poetry: "Sun=Sense=Less"

Whistling Fire: "The Art of Vibration"
With Painted Words: "Counting [on] Broken Rings"
Ygdrasil: "In Butterflied Dance"
            "Old McDonald's Algorithm"

About The Author

A.J. Huffman has published eleven solo chapbooks and one joint chapbook through various small presses. Her new full-length poetry collection, *Another Blood Jet,* is now available from Eldritch Press. She has another full-length poetry collection scheduled for release in Summer 2015, titled, *A Few Bullets Short of Home,* from mgv2>publishing. She is a Pushcart Prize nominee, and her poetry, fiction, and haiku have appeared in hundreds of national and international journals, including *Labletter, The James Dickey Review, Bone Orchard, EgoPHobia, Kritya*, and *Offerta Speciale*, in which her work appeared in both English and Italian translation. She is also the founding editor of Kind of a Hurricane Press. www.kindofahurricanepress.com.